Welcome to
THAILAND

Gareth Stevens Publishing
A WORLD ALMANAC EDUCATION GROUP COMPANY

Written by
JO WYNADEN/RONALD CHERRY

Edited in USA by
DOROTHY L. GIBBS

Designed by
LYNN CHIN

Picture research by
SUSAN JANE MANUEL

This edition first published in 2001 by
Gareth Stevens Publishing
A World Almanac Education Group Company
330 West Olive Street, Suite 100
Milwaukee, WI 53212 USA

Please visit our web site at:
www.garethstevens.com
For a free color catalog describing
Gareth Stevens' list of high-quality books
and multimedia programs, call
1-800-542-2595 (USA) or
1-800-461-9120 (CANADA).
Gareth Stevens Publishing's
Fax: (414) 332-3567.

© **TIMES MEDIA PRIVATE LIMITED 2001**
Originated and designed by
Times Editions
An imprint of Times Media Private Limited
A member of the Times Publishing Group
Times Centre, 1 New Industrial Road
Singapore 536196
http://www.timesone.com.sg/te

Library of Congress Cataloging-in-Publication Data
Wynaden, Jo.
Welcome to Thailand / Jo Wynaden and Ronald Cherry.
p. cm. — (Welcome to my country)
Includes bibliographical references and index.
ISBN 0-8368-2527-6 (lib. bdg.)
1. Thailand—Juvenile literature. [I. Thailand.]
I. Cherry, Ronald. II. Title. III. Series.
DS563.5.W96   2001
959.3—dc21   2001025018

Printed in Malaysia

1 2 3 4 5 6 7 8 9 05 04 03 02 01

PICTURE CREDITS
Bes Stock: cover, 5, 7, 9 (top), 17, 27 (top),
   34 (bottom), 38, 39, 43, 45
Michele Burgess: 8, 14
Blaine Harrington III: 4
The Hutchison Library: 3 (top), 20
John R. Jones: 33 (top)
Fiona Nichols/Times Editions: 15 (bottom)
Photobank Photolibrary: 2, 3 (bottom),
   6, 9 (bottom), 10, 12 (bottom), 13,
   15 (top), 16, 18, 19, 22, 26, 30 (both),
   31, 33 (bottom), 40 (both)
Pietro Scozzari: 21, 32, 41
David Simson: 28
Still Pictures: 3 (center), 36
Liba Taylor: 1, 23, 24, 34 (top), 35
Nik Wheeler: 11, 12 (top), 25, 27 (bottom),
   29, 37

Digital Scanning by Superskill Graphics Pte Ltd

Contents

Words that appear in the glossary are printed in **boldface** type the first time they occur in the text.

Welcome to Thailand!

Thailand is called the Land of Smiles. It is a nation of warm, friendly people and many different cultures. In spite of the modern technology available in this young country, most Thais lead traditional lifestyles. Let's learn about the Thais and their beautiful land.

Opposite: The products sold at Thailand's floating markets attract both Thais and tourists.

Below: The city of Surin is the elephant capital of Thailand and the site of the annual Elephant Roundup festival.

The Flag of Thailand

The current flag of Thailand was adopted in 1917. It has two red bands, two white bands, and one blue band. Red stands for the Thai nation. White represents Buddhism, which is the country's main religion. Blue represents Thailand's monarch, or king.

5

The Land

With an area of 198,115 square miles (513,118 square kilometers), Thailand is the third largest country in Southeast Asia. It has four separate regions — the central plain, the north, the northeast, and the south.

The central plain surrounds the Chao Phraya River, which is the country's most important waterway.

Below: Canals called *khlongs* (klongs) provide water for growing crops as well as for boat transportation.

Bangkok, Thailand's capital city, is also located in this region. The northern region has many mountains and contains the country's highest peak, Doi Inthanon, at 8,514 feet (2,595 meters). The northeastern region is called the Khorat Plateau. It is a dry area with poor soil. The south has jungles, beaches, and cliffs, as well as many important natural resources.

Above: The Phi Phi Islands in southern Thailand are surrounded by beautiful coral reefs and crystal clear waters.

Left: Thailand's tropical climate is ideal for growing orchids. Over 1,000 varieties of orchids grow there.

Climate

Thailand has a tropical climate with temperatures that generally range from 75° to 90° Fahrenheit (24° to 32° Celsius). In most areas, **monsoons** create a rainy season, a cool season, and a hot season. The south, however, is always hot.

Plants and Animals

The rain forests of Thailand have thousands of species of plants, including 3,000 kinds of **fungi** and 600 varieties of ferns.

The animals of Thailand include tigers, leopards, bears, elephants, rhinoceroses, and monkeys, as well as an abundance of sea life. Some of Thailand's animals are in danger of becoming extinct, so the government has established parks and other safe areas to protect them.

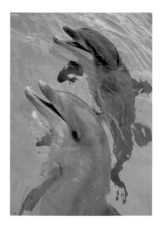

Above: Dolphins (*above*), dugongs, and whales are just a few of the hundreds of species of sea life in Thailand.

Left: Leatherback turtles come onto land only once each year to lay their eggs on the beach. This very large turtle is one of Thailand's endangered sea animals.

History

Little is known about the history of Thailand until about a thousand years ago, when the Tai people of China moved south into Siam, the area now called Thailand. At that time, the **Khmer** empire of Angkor controlled most of Siam.

In 1238, Tai leaders freed the city of Sukhothai from the Khmer and established the first Siamese kingdom.

Left: Before the thirteenth century, groups of Tais fought in many wars against both foreign kingdoms and each other.

Before the end of the century, the Tai people of the Sukhothai kingdom began to call themselves *Thai*. When this kingdom started to fall apart, it was taken over by the Ayutthaya kingdom.

Between 1351 and 1767, the Ayutthaya kingdom established good relationships with many countries in Asia and Europe. In 1767, however, this kingdom was invaded by Burma (now Myanmar).

Above: The temple Wat Mahathat was built when the city of Ayutthaya was the center of a **flourishing** and powerful kingdom.

Left: Thailand's present monarch, King Bhumibol Adulyadej, was crowned in 1946. Because he is a descendant of the Chakri dynasty, King Bhumibol is also known as Rama IX.

From Siam to Thailand

Soon after the kingdom of Ayutthaya collapsed, a Siamese official named Taksin became king. Taksin's army defeated Burma and conquered parts of Cambodia and Laos. In 1782, General Chao Phraya Mahakasatsuk succeeded Taksin as king of Siam. He became Rama I, the first king in the *Chakri* (chuk-kree) **dynasty**.

Below: King Rama I was named after the hero in *Ramakian* (rah-mah-kee-un), the Thai version of the Hindu epic, the *Ramayana*.

During the nineteenth century, some of the countries around Siam became European **colonies**. Under the rulers King Mongkut (r. 1851–1868) and King Chulalongkorn (r. 1868–1910), Siam remained the only free country in Southeast Asia.

In 1932, the Siamese government became a **constitutional monarchy**, which reduced the power of the king. In 1939, the country was renamed Thailand, meaning "Land of the Free."

Left: Siamese **delegates** often visited European courts, such as the court of French king Louis XIV. Good relations with France and Britain kept Siam from becoming a European colony in the nineteenth century.

World War II and Beyond

Wanting to control Asia, Japan invaded Thailand in 1941. To cooperate with Japan, Thailand declared war on the United States and Great Britain.

In 1946, after Bhumibol Adulyadej became king, Thailand joined the United Nations. Throughout the postwar period, the political power of the Thai military grew, and it is still a powerful force in Thailand's government today.

Above: This World War II memorial at Kanchanaburi honors the many thousands of Allied prisoners who died while building the bridge over the Khwae Noi River (River Kwai).

King Ramkhamhaeng
(r. 1279–1298)

As ruler of the Sukhothai kingdom, King Ramkhamhaeng became a powerful political leader. He also supported arts and literature and created the Thai alphabet.

King Chulalongkorn
(r. 1868–1910)

King Chulalongkorn

By building railways, roads, and hospitals, King Chulalongkorn helped modernize Siam. He also ended slavery, in 1905.

Chan and Mook

Chan and Mook

Dressed as male soldiers, Thai sisters Chan and Mook defeated a Burmese invasion of Phuket in 1875. King Rama V honored their bravery by giving them royal titles.

Government and the Economy

Thailand's constitutional monarchy is governed by the National Assembly, which consists of a Senate and a House of Representatives. A prime minister is the head of government.

Thailand is divided into seventy-six *changwat* (*chang-waht*), or provinces. Each province is headed by a governor.

Below: The king of Thailand has a limited role in government. As head of state, he calls together the meetings of the National Assembly.

Left: The military plays a leading role in Thailand's political and social issues. Former generals and **admirals** head most of the country's political parties.

International Relations

Thailand is on friendly terms with countries all over the world, especially the United States, France, and Britain. Since 1954, Thailand has been the headquarters for the Southeast Asia Treaty Organization (SEATO). It is also one of the original members of the Association of Southeast Asian Nations (ASEAN).

The Economy

Over half of Thailand's workforce is employed in agriculture. Main crops include rice, rubber, and **copra**.

Tourism and mining metals such as tin and zinc are among Thailand's biggest industries. Recently, the manufacturing industry has been growing, too.

Above: Many of the people living in Thailand's coastal areas earn a living by fishing.

Growth and Decline

Until the late 1990s, the steady and rapid growth of business and foreign **investments** in Thailand meant jobs and **prosperity** for the Thai people. When the Southeast Asian economy slowed down in 1997, however, many businesses in Thailand were forced to close, and many people lost their jobs.

By 1999, the Thai economy was improving again, but it will be years before it is as strong as it had been in the 1980s and early 1990s.

Below:
The low cost of labor in Thailand has helped make industries, such as automobile parts manufacturing more successful.

People and Lifestyle

Although the people of Thailand come from many different **ethnic** groups, all of the country's citizens are called *Thai*. Minority groups include the Chinese, the Malays, and some hill tribes.

Most Chinese-Thai live in cities, especially in Bangkok, where many of their ancestors, who were Chinese

Below: Religion is important to the Thai people. For most Buddhists, the temple is at the center of community life.

20

immigrants, settled about two hundred years ago. Bangkok has a special Chinatown area.

The Malays, who live mostly in the south, are related to the people of Malaysia. They speak both Malay and Thai, and they are Muslims.

Six hill tribes live in the north and northeast regions of Thailand. These tribes originally came from southern China, Laos, and Myanmar.

Above: The Lisu hill tribe came to Thailand from eastern Tibet in 1921. Other hill tribes include the Akha, Hmong, Yao, Lahu, and Karen.

The Family

Thai families are usually large. Many generations often live in the same household. Some members of Thai families are not even related.

From a very young age, Thais are taught to respect everyone older than themselves, as well as people in positions of power. Respect is shown with a traditional Buddhist greeting

Above: A nuclear family in Thailand is rare. Most Thai families include many relatives. Some even include non-relatives. The non-relatives are called "aunt" or "uncle" by other family members.

called the *wai* (why). This gesture is done by bowing the head and raising the hands, with the palms pressed together, in front of the chin.

Women in Thailand

Women are important in Thailand. They manage households and raise children, often while working in businesses or industries, too.

Below: Children learn to wai at a very young age. Forgetting to wai to elders is considered rude.

Education

Thailand has had a modern public education system since the late 1800s. Children must attend school from the age of seven until they are fourteen. Public schools are free, but parents must pay for school uniforms and most supplies. Nearly seven million children attend elementary school in Thailand each year. Less than one million of them, however, go on to high school.

Below: Although elementary school is required, most Thai children leave school at the age of fourteen to find jobs and help support their families.

Competition to attend a university in Thailand is fierce. The country has more than thirty universities, but each one can admit only a few hundred new students. High school students must take a national examination to get a place at a university. Students with the highest scores can choose to study law, engineering, or medicine at any of the universities.

Above: During lunch breaks, Thai students enjoy time with their classmates.

Religion

Buddhism is the official religion of Thailand. About 95 percent of the population are Buddhists. Thai Buddhists worship at a *wat* (waht), or temple. The wat is the center of life in every village and community.

Although most Chinese-Thai are Buddhists, they also practice Taoist traditions. Taoism teaches people to lead simple, honest lives.

Left: The Grand Palace in Bangkok is home to the Wat Phra Keo, which holds the Emerald Buddha. To the Thais, the Emerald Buddha is the most important Buddhist image in the world.

Left: *Visakha Bucha* (vee-sah-kah boo-chah) is the most sacred Buddhist festival in Thailand.

About 4 percent of Thai people are Muslims. Thai Muslims live mainly in southern Thailand. They are descendants of traders from the Middle East, Indonesia, Malaysia, and India. Thailand also has small numbers of Christians and Hindus.

Thailand's hill tribes practice **animism**, which is worshiping the spirits of nature.

Below: Muslims will find mosques in any of Thailand's larger cities.

Language

The national language of Thailand is called "Thai." It is believed to be a form of Chinese that developed over many centuries. Actually, several different Thai languages developed. The official language of schools and the government is Central Thai.

Left: Street signs in Thailand usually appear only in Thai. These signs are telling motorists to wear seat belts and to follow all traffic regulations.

Literature

Thai literature dates back to the 1200s, but the most famous story is probably the classic epic poem *Ramakian*, from the eighteenth century.

Since the 1920s, Thai journalists and novelists, such as Kukrit Pramoj, Dok Mai Sot, and Kulap Saipradit, have made important contributions to Thai literature.

Above:
A large selection of magazines and newspapers are sold at newsstands all over Thailand.

Arts

Theater in Thailand is both classical and traditional. Classical theater is an older form that is rarely performed today. Traditional theater is more popular and is performed often in both cities and **rural** areas.

The *khon* (kohn) is one form of classical theater. Actors in masks and elaborate costumes perform without speaking. They are accompanied by a traditional Thai orchestra.

Above: In a khon performance, the actors onstage move silently to words spoken by a narrator.

Left: These Thai girls are students at a dance school in Bangkok.

Lakhon (lah-kohn) is another form of classical theater. Lakhon performers are also accompanied by music and songs, but they speak onstage and do not wear masks. Both kohn and lakhon performances are based on stories from the *Ramakian* and on Thai folktales.

The most common form of traditional theater is *likay* (lee-kay). Unlike the classical forms, likay is comedy. The actors are loud, and they often **interact** with the audience.

Thai Music

Classical Thai music is played on traditional Thai instruments, such as a *khlui* (klwee), or wooden flute, and a *thon* (tohn), or double hand drum. Thai orchestras typically play at social events and theater performances.

Village folk music has existed in Thailand for hundreds of years, and it is still an important part of festivals and temple ceremonies.

Below: Members of a school band in Thailand play trombones and other modern instruments.

Rock, jazz, and pop music are also popular in Thailand. King Bhumibol himself is a jazz composer and plays the saxophone and clarinet.

Above: Decorative Thai woodcarvings display detailed patterns of angels, dragons, and lotus flowers.

Religious Art

Centuries ago, paintings, sculptures, and woodcarvings were used both to decorate temples and to teach people about Buddhism. Some images of the Buddha that were carved or sculpted in the sixth century still exist today.

Leisure

Thais enjoy relaxing with family and friends. When they go out somewhere, they usually go in large groups that include people of all different ages. Watching movies and eating out at restaurants are popular activities in **urban** areas. In rural areas, friends get together to play cards, watch television, or just visit. Teenagers enjoy picnics with groups of friends.

Above: Tai Chi is one of many types of exercise popular among Thais.

Left: Some of the movies shown in Thailand are made locally, but most come from places such as Hong Kong.

A Thai picnic means lots of food and at least one guitar, so the group can sing together.

Above: Thai kites are made out of bamboo and paper. Some kites are very large and colorful.

Kite Flying

Kite flying is a sport that started centuries ago. Thais fly kites all year long, but competitions are held in February, March, and April, which are months when monsoons provide the strongest winds.

Sports

Soccer, basketball, badminton, tennis, and volleyball are some of Thailand's favorite sports. *Takraw* (tah-kraw) is a traditional Thai game played with a small **rattan** ball. Thais play three kinds of takraw — net takraw, circle takraw, and basket takraw. In all three, players are allowed to use any part of the body, except their hands, to keep the ball in the air.

Below: Takraw games are often played in public parks. Net takraw is very similar to volleyball.

Muay Thài (moo-ay tie), or Thai kickboxing, is another popular sport. It is a martial art that combines tae kwon do and boxing.

Animal competitions, such as cockfights, bullfights, and buffalo races, are ancient sports, but they are still popular in some rural areas of Thailand. Animals as small as beetles may be trained to fight.

Above:
In Thailand, kick-boxing is as popular as soccer is across Europe. Kickboxers use their feet, knees, and elbows, as well as their fists.

Buddhist Festivals

Many holidays and festivals in Thailand celebrate special events in the life of the Buddha. The most important Buddhist holiday, Visakha Bucha, takes place in late May or early June. This festival celebrates the Buddha's birth, day of **enlightenment**, and death. *Khao Pansa* (kow pun-sah), the Buddhist season of Lent, lasts from July to October. During this time, Thai Buddhists pay special attention to prayer and worship, and Thai men and boys often become Buddhist monks.

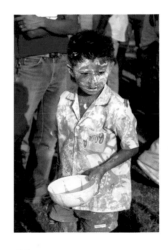

Above:
Traditionally, people sprinkled water on each other during Songkran, believing it would bring rain. Today, Songkran is noisy and wet. Children and adults go into the streets and throw bowls or buckets of water at each other. They throw flour, too

Other Thai Festivals

Loy Krathong (loy krah-tohng) is a colorful celebration held after the rice harvest, usually in November. This festival thanks the water spirits for the water they provided during the growing season. The Thai New Year, or *Songkran* (sohng-krahn), is celebrated from April 13 to April 15.

Opposite:
Loy Krathong is celebrated all over Thailand, but the biggest celebrations are in Sukhothai.

Food

Thai food has a taste that combines sweet, sour, salty, and spicy hot flavors. The most well-known Thai dishes are **curries**. Spicy coconut-milk soups, grilled chicken and pork, and stir-fried vegetables are also favorites.

Rice is the most important food in the Thai diet. It is served at almost every meal along with flavorful meat, fruit, and vegetable dishes.

Above: A touch of artistry is often added to the fruits and vegetables served with Thai dishes. Some are carved to look like flowers or boats.

Left: Fresh vegetables are an important part of Thai **cuisine**. Because they must be chopped, sliced, and ground, some Thai dishes take a long time to prepare.

40

Fruits are in season all year round. Thais enjoy all kinds of tropical fruits, such as bananas, mangoes, papayas, pineapples, and coconuts.

Thailand is famous for durians. These fruits, which can be found only in Southeast Asia, are very expensive and have an unpleasant smell. The creamy white or yellow fruit inside their prickly green shells, however, is healthful and delicious.

Above: Crispy pancakes are a type of fast food in Thailand. They are often sold at the floating markets.

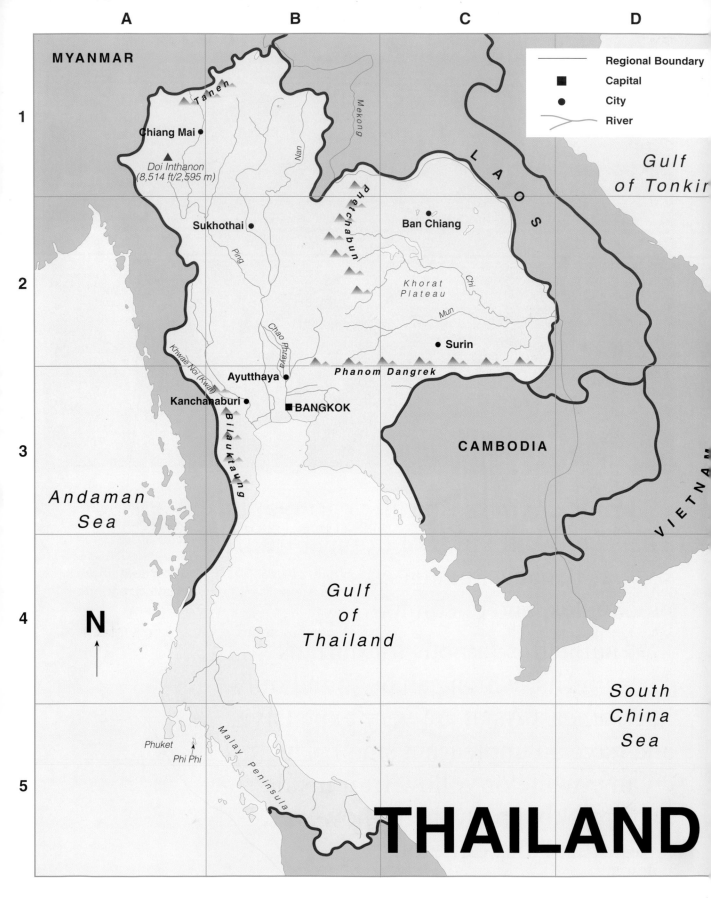

Above: Bangkok has many modern buildings and skyscrapers.

Andaman Sea A2–B5

Ayutthaya B3

Ban Chiang C2

Bangkok B3

Bilauktaung Mountains B3

Cambodia C3–D3

Chao Phraya River B2–B3

Chi River C2

Chiang Mai A1

Doi Inthanon A1

Gulf of Thailand B3–C5

Gulf of Tonkin D1–D2

Kanchanaburi B3

Khorat Plateau C2

Khwae Noi (Kwai) River A2–B3

Laos B1–D3

Malay Peninsula B5

Mekong River B1–D4

Mun River B2–C2

Myanmar A1–B4

Nan River B1–B2

Phanom Dangrek Mountains B2–C2

Phetchabun Mountains B1–B2

Phi Phi Islands A5

Phuket Island A5

Ping River B1–B2

South China Sea D4–D5

Sukhothai B2

Surin C2

Tanen Mountains A1–B1

Vietnam C1–D4

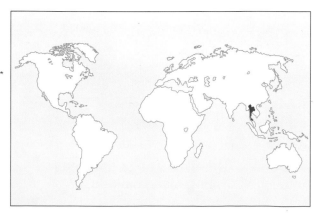

Quick Facts

Official Name   Kingdom of Thailand

Capital   Bangkok

Official Language   Thai

Population   61,230,874 (2000 estimate)

Land Area   198,115 square miles (513,118 square km)

Highest Point   Doi Inthanon 8,514 feet (2,595 m)

Major Rivers   Chao Phraya, Mekong

Main Religion   Buddhism

Major Festivals   Visakha Bucha

Khao Pansa

Loy Krathong

Songkran

Ethnic Groups   Thai 75%, Chinese 14%, others 11%

Main Exports   Computers and parts, rice, textiles

Main Imports   Consumer goods, fuels

Currency   Baht (37.8 baht = U.S. $1 as of 2000)

Opposite: This Thai boy is dressed in Shan costume to participate in the Handicraft Festival in Chiang Mai, Thailand.

Glossary

admirals: top commanders in a navy or over fleets of ships.

animism: the belief that all natural organisms have souls.

Chakri (chuk-kree): the name of the currently ruling Thai dynasty.

colonies: countries or areas that are controlled by another country.

constitutional monarchy: a system of government in which a king or sovereign ruler of a nation exercises power according to the laws of an established constitution.

copra: dried coconut meat.

cuisine: a style of preparing and cooking food.

curries: meat or vegetable dishes seasoned with curry powder and other East Indian spices.

delegates: people chosen to act for or represent another person or country, especially at a political meeting.

dynasty: a family of rulers who inherit their power.

enlightenment: a state of highly developed intelligence or spiritual understanding.

ethnic: related to a certain race or culture of people.

flourishing: growing and developing quickly; successful.

fungi: plants, such as mushrooms and molds, that are not green and have no leaves or flowers.

interact: communicate with other people while working or spending time together.

investments: money given, or loaned, to help businesses grow so they can return greater amounts of money.

Khmer: the native people of Cambodia.

monsoons: strong seasonal winds.

nuclear family: a father, a mother, and their children.

prosperity: wealth or success.

Ramakian (rah-mah-kee-un): a famous Thai epic poem about good and evil, based on the *Ramayana*, a classic Hindu epic.

rattan: the tough straw or canelike stems of Asian palm plants often woven into baskets or wickerwork.

rural: related to the countryside.

urban: related to cities or towns.

More Books to Read

Asia for Younger Readers: Thailand.
    Jennifer Sharples (Success Media)

Bangkok. Cities of the World series.
    Sylvia McNair (Children's Press)

Buddhist Temple. Places of Worship
    series. Angela Wood
    (Gareth Stevens)

Even a Little Is Something: Stories of
    Nong. Tom Glass (Linnet Books)

Family in Thailand. Families the World
    Over series. Ruth and Neil
    Thomson (Lerner)

The Girl Who Wore Too Much:
    A Folktale from Thailand.
    Margaret Read MacDonald
    (August House Little Folk)

A Tale of Two Rice Birds.
    Clare Hodgson Meeker
    (Sasquatch Books)

Thailand. Countries of the World
    series. Kristin Thoennes
    (Bridgestone Books)

Thailand. Festivals of the World series.
    Harlinah Whyte (Gareth Stevens)

Videos

North Thailand & Laos.
    (Lonely Planet)

Royal Families of the World: Japan,
    Thailand, Morocco, Jordan.
    (Goldhil Home Media)

Thailand. (Education 2000)

Thailand: Jewel of the Orient.
    The Living Edens series.
    (PBS Home Video)

Web Sites

www.amazing-thailand.com

www.escati.com/thailand_of_escati.htm

www.interknowledge.com/thailand/

www.sriwittayapaknam.ac.th/

Due to the dynamic nature of the Internet, some web sites stay current longer than others. To find additional web sites, use a reliable search engine with one or more of the following keywords to help you locate information about Thailand. Keywords: *Adulyadej, Bangkok, Buddhism, Mekong River,* Ramakian, *Siam, Thailand.*

Index